Making a Case Your Donors Will Love

The Secret to Selling the Dream

MAKING A CASE YOUR DONORS WILL LOVE

The Secret to Selling the Dream

JEROLD PANAS

First printed in June 2014

Printed in the United States of America

This text is printed on acid-free paper.

Emerson & Church, Publishers
15 Brook Street—Medfield, MA 02052
Tel. 508-359-0019—Fax 508-359-2703
www.emersonandchurch.com

Library of Congress Cataloging-in-Publication Data

Panas, Jerold.
Making a case your donors will love : the secret to selling the dream / Jerold Panas.
pages cm
ISBN 978-1-889102-52-8 (pbk. : alk. paper) 1. Fund raising. 2. Endowments. 3. Charities—Management. 4. Nonprofit organizations—Management. I. Title.
HV41.2.P357 2014
658.15'224—dc23
2014011050

Contents

"There is not much to be said about
the period, except that most writers
don't reach it soon enough."

—Edith Wharton

CHAPTER 1

"Words are, of course, the most powerful drug used by mankind."
—*Rudyard Kipling*

The Magic of the Word

I had just finished talking with Virginia Piper about a new science building for Xavier High School in Phoenix. One of the most charming individuals I've ever met, Virginia had a glow and a smile that gave hope in February.

Let me take you back.

I'm in Virginia's living room waxing eloquent about the proposed science center. Trouble is, it's only of modest interest to her. It's really the mission and the program of the school that fascinate Virginia. She loves the fact that it's all girls, the emphasis on rigorous scholarship, and most of all the focus on developing leadership in young women.

"Do you have something to leave so I can read more about the school?" she asks.

It's only personal style, but I don't like trotting out printed material until I've made the presentation. Sometimes I don't even do that. I prefer putting it in the mail for the probable donor to read, including a letter thanking him or her for the visit. It's a powerful reinforcement.

I hand Virginia the case statement. I wouldn't typically do that, but she asks a second time.

The case is called "The 7th Hour," a title with special significance to the school.

"May I take a moment to read it now?" Virginia asks.

I consider this an excellent augury. If she were tepid about the project, she could simply have asked me to leave it behind. And usher me out the door.

Something extraordinary starts to happen as she reads. The case gets a headlock on her. She loves it. She reads some passages out loud to me.

Virginia excuses herself and goes into her study off the living room. When she returns a few minutes later, she hands me a check.

I peek at it, trying not to be too obvious. Good grief! It's a check for $50,000.

"I'm so impressed with the story of Xavier I want to be a part of the program."

I hand the check back (we're actually hoping to ask for a much larger gift on the next visit).

Virginia insists I take it, but we schedule a second visit, this time with Sister Joan, head of the school.

You can guess the rest, I'm sure. Visit Xavier today, and you'll see the Virginia Piper Science Center prominently centered on campus.

My point—and the reason I wrote this book—is that no matter how dazzling the oral presentation—and, forgive me, but mine was stellar that day—you still need to describe the need in writing and substantiate why your institution is uniquely positioned to fulfill it. You can see the power it had over Virginia.

Chances are you have within you what Tennessee Williams called, "A great dammed-up emotional ebullience." My hope is that these pages will unleash those feelings and help you produce a case you'll take surging pride in.

Your charge is to sell your dream with all the conviction and ardor within you.

When the reader says, "I believe," you'll know you've done the job.

CHAPTER 2

"We are all apprentices in a craft where
no one ever becomes a master."
—Ernest Hemingway

Dance with the Bears

I'm not a writer.

That's what makes me a good choice to write about case statements.

Let me explain.

I don't earn my bread and board with a pen, but I love to write. Long ago I found in me *cacoethes scribendi*—the urge to scribble.

Sure, I've written case statements—scores of them. And I've edited, well, close to a thousand. That's no exaggeration.

But here's what's more important. I'm the one who actually has to use a case. I review them with leaders when I conduct feasibility studies and when calling on likely donors.

In a sense, I walk the talk, as they say.

As you'll learn in these pages, an effective case seizes readers by the collar. It inspires and motivates them to go from their minds to their hearts to their checkbooks. To do that you need writing that's so stirring you can, as Flaubert said, "Bang out tunes that could make bears dance."

In this book, I guide you through each step. You'll find that sometimes I disagree with what others have written. That's because most articles and books on case statements are written by writers, not by users.

But even when my advice differs from what you've been doing or have been taught, I promise it's like Brussels sprouts: they're good for you even though you don't like them.

The effective case, like a Bach partita, begins by breaking the silence and ends by returning to it. It leaves everything in between completely and pleasingly resolved.

Come along. You and I are going to make some beautiful music together.

CHAPTER 3

"Any fool can know. The point is to understand."

—*Albert Einstein*

Know Your Reader

Not long ago we completed a case for a seminary in the southwest. The manuscript was approved by the president and several board members. It didn't quite have the allure of 007's exploits, but it possessed a certain pace and passion.

We send it for review to the person who's likely to be the seminary's largest donor. In no time she emails me: "This is a weak case—one of the weakest I've read. It's only my opinion but I think it should be rewritten without so many adjectives and adverbs."

I don't have to attend a seminar on *Writing a Case* to know I'm in serious trouble. It's like being between a dog and the lamppost. You know the feeling.

My first reaction is to defend the piece. I feel like my old high school Latin teacher protecting the punch bowl at the prom. But of course I realize we have to make drastic changes. In fact, our writer starts all over from scratch.

The new draft is straightforward. No adjectives, no adverbs. It reads like the social notes of a Methodist Church newsletter.

We submit it to our prospective donor, and she loves it. Loves it!

We then send it to the president and several members of the board. They love it, too. Somewhere in the background, I hear the theme from *Rocky.*

I learn an important lesson. While I wanted this case to have sparkle and shine, that's not what the president and largest donors wanted. I should have taken a better measure of them before preparing it.

It's critical to know your market. Hundreds of copies of the case will be distributed. Perhaps thousands. But keep in mind you're pulling out the stops for an audience of . . . one.

You need to have a solid sense of who that person is. You must also be aware of your many constituencies, as I discuss in the next chapter.

CHAPTER 4

"For me, it is far better to grasp the Universe
as it really is than to persist in delusion,
however satisfying and reassuring."

—*Carl Sagan*

One Suit Doesn't Fit All

For years I've prepared and furnished clients with case statements. Some were downright dazzling and some, well, less so.

But it's only in the past few years I've fully realized that the same case, no matter how brilliant, can't be effective with all constituencies.

Take a hospital. The case you prepare for former patients doesn't have the same importance and impact on the medical staff. And former donors and nurses—they don't react in the same way nor have the same imperatives or incentives.

Here's a sample of the various constituencies of a typical hospital. I've listed twelve distinct groups. There may be more. Each has its own interests, its own characteristics, and its own degrees of provincialism.

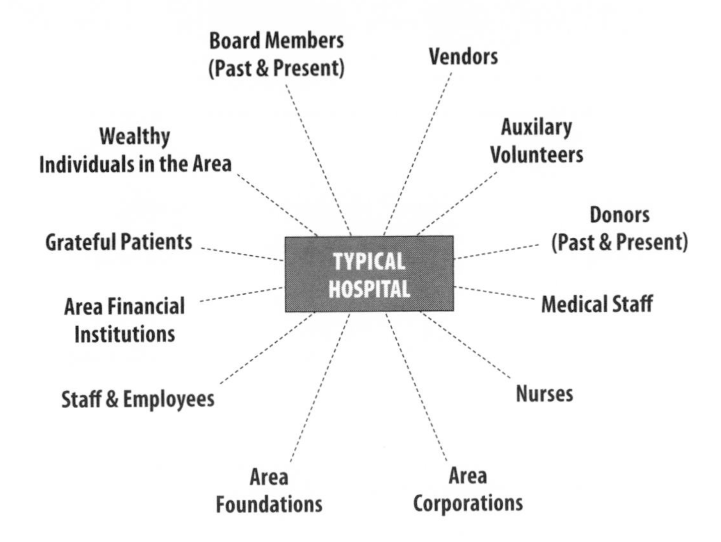

Similarly, the typical college has different constituencies:

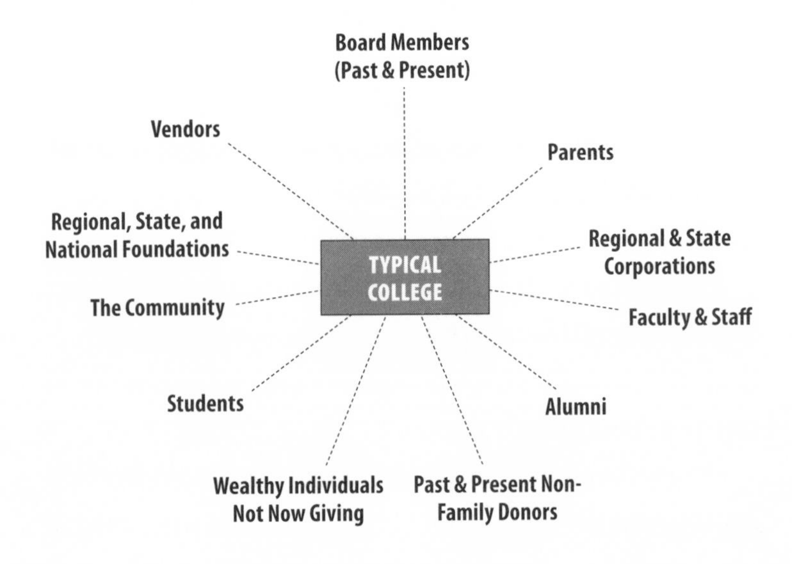

It's like buying clothes. One suit doesn't fit all. One case may do the overarching job for several of your constituencies. But for some special groups, you're going to want a piece that focuses distinctively on them.

We did the case for Fisk University, a historically black college. Fisk is a wonderful school. It has one of the greatest art collections of any college in the country. Sadly, that's a fact unknown even to many in Nashville.

I prepare what I consider a heartfelt case. It has passion, energy, and vision for the future. I'm delighted with the results and present it to the president. He reads the case and hands it back.

"The grammar is terrible," he says.

Here we go again.

I mention that God doesn't much care about bad grammar. "That may be true," the president shoots back, "but He doesn't take any pleasure in it, either."

The president continues: "You don't understand, Jerry. I can live with incomplete sentences and contractions. I see what you're trying to do. But keep in mind how some of our prospects might perceive Fisk.

"I want them to think of us as a small Harvard right here in Nashville—with the highest-quality education and the most scholarly faculty anywhere. Our material has to reflect that."

The president is absolutely right. I applied my creativity and energy to what I thought would motivate a donor. I gave scant thought to how the college would wish to be perceived.

We end up writing four cases for Fisk. One is for the president's "elite" group of major donors. It doesn't have the snap-crackle-pop of our original, but it's infallibly correct.

The second is for key community leaders and probable donors in the Nashville area. They have no relationship to Fisk. But they have great civic pride and feel the university is an important asset.

And there is one for the faculty and staff. We want them to know and be able to tell the important story.

Finally, there is the case we prepare for the alumni. In this one, we lead them by the hand back to the campus. "Just think for a moment of the wondrous ways Fisk has touched your life. . . ."

You might think that four cases for a school with fewer than 600 students is overkill. But it isn't. Knowing your constituency is part of the secret. That and being aware of how the institution's ethos and character should be conveyed.

CHAPTER 5

> "Be above it! Make the world serve your purpose, but do not serve it!"
>
> —*Goethe*

The Powerful Seven

I'm reminded of the story of the king's royal archers. They're returning from a particularly bad day of practice and drill. Not one bull's-eye in three hours. The master archer gives them a royal tongue-lashing.

On the way back to the castle, they spot a youngster—no more than ten years old. He's shooting at the side of a barn. There are eight targets and an arrow precisely in the middle, each in the bull's-eye.

The master archer has all of his men dismount. He says to the lad, "Show these supposedly great archers how to hold a bow and arrow and hit a bull's-eye."

"It's easy," said the youngster. "I shoot at the barn. Then I draw a target around the arrow."

Unlike that young archer, you do have a target to hit with your case. Actually, as noted in the previous chapter, you may have several targets, depending on your constituencies.

But regardless of the number, I want to share with you now seven significant ways your case should be used.

1. **To seek agreement.** The case secures commitment among your primary leaders and board members. Everyone must agree and have a solid understanding of the organization's objectives and long-term goals. At times this is more difficult than it may seem.

   We were engaged by the CEO of one of the nation's most highly regarded cancer centers. "We're getting ready for a huge capital campaign," he tells us. "I want a case that's stirring."

   What we produced sizzled. It set off sparks. And it nearly singed the future of the CEO.

   The problem was he had no consensus from his board about the project he asked us to anchor the case around. One board member we interviewed told us, "I knew absolutely nothing about this project. We had no inkling. More than that, I don't think it's a very good idea. I'm damn upset."

2. **As a roadmap.** The case provides direction and a defined strategy to your primary constituencies. It becomes an expert witness for how you will achieve your mission.
3. **To describe results.** The case informs leaders and workers of the need and of your audacious dreams. It demonstrates and substantiates how the success of the endeavor will work to the immense and unending benefit of those you serve.

   You needn't be modest here. You're creating magical castles in the air. Your case lays the foundation for them.
4. **To broaden the circle.** The effective case enlists new friends and leaders to your cause. Even those who may not have been familiar with you before reading the case are caught in your web. That's your job. You demonstrate how their investment produces untold benefits and results. It's an irresistible call to action.
5. **To win over donors.** The case is an early working document and cultivation piece for prospective major donors. I love using it this way. Let major donors know your case is still in draft form—a work in progress—and that you want them to be among the first to review it and suggest changes.

I send along a letter that reads something like this: "I am so pleased we're going to get together. Before our visit I'd like to ask you to take a few minutes to read about this new program. The enclosed piece isn't final yet, and I want your reaction. Mark up your copy or circle any areas that you may wish to discuss." I even send a red pen with the letter.

What I find is that when top donors are asked to read the draft, with a request to help evaluate and perhaps edit the story, they actually read it. Used this way, a case is wonderfully engaging.

6. **To carry the flag.** The case is a document that helps readers endorse and share your vision. They accept a greater and ever-expanding responsibility of identifying with your invincible mission. They understand your loftiest aspirations. Robert Frost called it "that immense energy of life which sparks a fire."
7. **To serve as a wellspring.** Nothing happens until you first describe the dream. Then the case becomes the sourcebook and guide for the writing of subsequent publications, articles, foundation proposals, and video presentations.

Did you notice something about this list? I didn't once mention money. What? No talk of money?

At some point in the case, of course, you have to talk about how much the dream is going to cost. A case statement is after all a vision with dollar signs. But that's not your focus.

Instead, your case is about challenges, about new ideas in confrontation with the old. You define the objectives, dispel questions, propel actions. You light the candles.

Or to put it more rudimentarily: The case isn't about leading a horse to water. It's all about making the equine thirsty.

CHAPTER 6

"Out of clutter, find simplicity."
—*Albert Einstein*

Hold the Light for Others to See

You are now ready to plan the formatting of your case. The French have a term, *mise en place*. It means all the pieces are in proper and perfect order. In truth, some may overlap, some may be repeated, and some may work best for you in a different order than I recommend. But you'll determine that along the way.

Let's examine the pieces one by one.

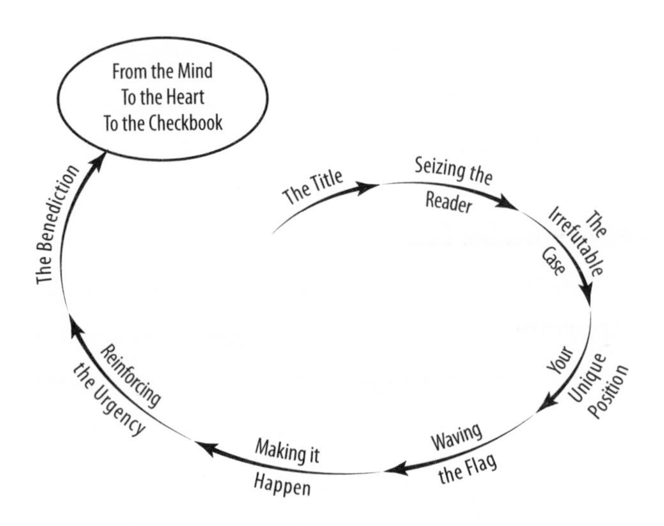

The Title

The title develops the theme and tone. Its inexorable job is to propel donors to turn to page one and your opening paragraphs.

Don't hold back. Your title should light the sky with fireworks.

Seizing the Reader

Your introductory paragraphs must create an irresistible bridge to the rest of your case. If you lose the reader here, you won't get him or her back. Often, a compelling quote in the early part of the case is effective.

Write these introductory paragraphs in a way that the reader can't escape your grasp. "Come with me. We're about to visit with some people you'll never forget, . . . I'll take you by the hand."

You cannot begin this journey without leaving footprints. Your readers will follow because you've marked the way.

➪ The Irrefutable Case

Here you describe the need and the reason for urgency. It's important the case become bigger and even more significant than your organization. (I'll explain later.)

You demonstrate in this section that your case is relevant. You make certain it has dramatic and emotional appeal. Most important, there must be a sense of urgency. Time won't wait. Double thunder!

This is where your case takes flight. If you want your reader to be with you on the landing, make certain they're involved on the takeoff.

➪ Your Unique Position

This section describes how your institution is uniquely positioned to meet the need head-on. You are first and last. No other group touches lives the way you do. You burn yourself into the hearts and minds of your readers.

➪ Waving the Flag

Here you describe the strength of your organization, its history, and mission. It would be easy to stumble here. You'll need to go to great lengths in this section to make your copy come alive. Your mission is your guiding anchor, but if it's dry or weighty it won't make the heart race.

➪ Reinforcing the Urgency

This reminds the reader of how pressing the need is. It must be addressed at once. Martin Luther King called it, "The fierce urgency of now." Remember, it's not about your organization. It's about those you serve. "Every 40 seconds we lose a child to malaria. We cannot linger, we cannot wait. . . ."

➪ Making It Happen

This describes what will be required financially to address the need. The case expresses your dreams and vision with a dollar sign. You're successful when your reader says, "I believe."

➪ The Benediction

This provides the close and final blessing to the program. The theme, which has been used selectively, and seductively, throughout, is employed once more for emphasis. You close with psalms of passionate wonder and celebration.

In the chapters that follow, I describe each of these elements in more detail. Don't worry about making each a separate segment in your writing. You probably shouldn't. Each will tend to meld together.

CHAPTER 7

"Think little goals and expect little achievements. Think big goals and win big success."

—David Joseph Schwartz

Bigger Than Your Organization

You've read in a professional journal or book that the case for your project should be bigger than the organization itself. But exactly what does that mean? It's like when writing teachers admonish their students to "show, not tell." A vague directive.

Here's how I understand it.

A while back, we were raising money for the Tampa Museum of Art. The community was being asked to provide funds to build a glorious new edifice, downtown on the Hillsborough River.

At last the museum would be able to exhibit its full collection. It would bring out of storage enrapturing pieces it didn't have the space to exhibit.

This new facility, it was estimated, would attract an additional 200,000 people each year.

But the case for this new building was far more powerful and compelling than just concrete and steel. For the first time, the museum would be able to invite young people by the busloads. We asked readers to picture those grade-school kids lining up at the entrance. Eager. Curious. Starry-eyed. See them working the hands-on displays. The whoop and waggle. It'll be glorious.

So the case was for the young people of the area.

But there's more.

The museum is on a gorgeous site on the river. Think of some of the positive environmental issues at play. The new building would enhance the River Walk. There would be local flora and fauna down to the river. A rather commonplace section of the Hillsborough River would be transformed into something endlessly inspirational.

But wait. The miracle isn't yet finished. There's still more.

The museum would bring thousands of families back into a fatigued downtown. It would be the centerpiece of a new cultural and arts area. It would reinvigorate and transform downtown. Anyone with a modicum of care, civic pride, and responsibility for the Tampa area had to support this project, regardless of his or her interest in art.

And, finally, think of this. There would be an infusion of money and people for the downtown merchants.

You understand my thrust here. All of a sudden, the program becomes of much greater and magnified consequence than simply creating a facility to house more art.

And that's your charge as a writer. You search for every felicitous possibility that makes the project more expansive and worthy than the organization itself.

It's your job to put it all into a package and develop an undeniable, irresistible, and urgent case for support.

Years ago I learned a lesson myself in finding the soul of the case.

The *Potomac* was Franklin D. Roosevelt's yacht. He used it regularly throughout his presidency—especially during World War II. It was his release.

Some significant meetings took place on the yacht—with Churchill, Eisenhower, King George VI and Queen Elizabeth, the prime minister of Canada, and on a number of occasions FDR's war cabinet.

The yacht would cruise up and down the Potomac River, for no more than a stretch of two or three miles. And then back again.

During the stressful and weary days of the war, the

dateline of news stories and radio broadcasts regularly carried the identification *From the Presidential Yacht Potomac.* You couldn't grow up in that era without feeling the yacht was part of your life.

When Roosevelt died, the *Potomac* was put in dry dock. Then not long after the war, a year or two perhaps, President Truman sold the yacht. In fact it went through several owners and was even renamed.

Finally, the yacht was purchased by a nonprofit group and in a special ceremony, rechristened *The Presidential Yacht Potomac.*

The boat was in terrible shape, needing to be completely renovated and made seaworthy. We were asked to raise funds to restore it. Jimmy Roosevelt, the president's son, chaired the campaign. Lucky me. I had an opportunity to work with history.

The case, which I had a hand in writing, was, pardon my immodesty, darn good. There were oversize drawings of each level of the ship and the architect's rendering of what it would look like. I wrote in words that glowed and glistened about how the yacht would be brought back to pristine and seaworthy condition.

But to my great discomfort, something was wrong. The people we approached for gifts were underwhelmed. This was a storied piece of history, I wanted to scream out, but it didn't seem to matter.

It was Clark Clifford, a wealthy Washington attorney, who gave me the clue.

He had been under secretary of state in Roosevelt's administration, and a close friend of the president. We called on him for a gift.

"You folks don't have this right at all," he said. "This program isn't about the restoration of a not-very-pretty boat.

"It's about FDR. About an exalted president. About the most exciting, dynamic, and fearful period in this nation's history.

"Rewrite this damn thing and come back and see me."

I felt like a scorned Job, scraping my scabs, penitent and pleading: "Why me, oh Lord—why me?" But rewrite it we did.

The new case we produced was full of photos of FDR. There were reprints of some newspaper headlines that carried the dateline *From the Presidential Yacht Potomac.*

We used no architectural drawings. No display of the proposed renovation. No pictures of the yacht itself. The case was replete with photos of history.

And guess what? It was an immense hit. And it was quite clear donors gave to the Office of the President and to the memory of FDR—not to the restoration of a boat.

Crusty old Clark Clifford—he made a leading gift.

CHAPTER 8

"The business schools reward difficult complex behavior more than simple behavior, but simple behavior is more effective."

—*Warren Buffett*

Why Should I Invest?

Mark is a venture capitalist, a highly successful one. I'm with him and his wife, Sheila, discussing the independent school their youngster attends in a suburb of Boston.

The family loves the school. "It's changed our son's life," Mark says. "It's just wonderful," Sheila beams.

"But this prospectus you gave us doesn't do it justice," says Mark. "I mean this constructively, but it's pretty weak."

You've probably guessed this isn't a propitious start! Mark's words become the fingernails on my chalkboard.

"The truth is," he continues, "if this was a business, I wouldn't invest." Being a venture capitalist, he thinks of the case as being a business prospectus. In a real sense it is.

This isn't my firm's case, I'm happy to say. Our writer made a first attempt that I thought was good. But the school's leadership felt we misunderstood the character of the school and failed to capture its ethos. They thought what we'd done was too long, too wordy. They called it tumid. (I had to look up the word, but I was pretty sure it wasn't positive.)

The headmaster took over and wrote the case from scratch. His is the document I'm now sharing with Mark.

Regardless of who wrote it, it's not acceptable to Mark.

As a venture capitalist, like any potential donor, he has four questions, and this case isn't answering them to his satisfaction:

1. Why should I invest in this organization? Does its mission align with my objectives?
2. Why should I invest in this project? Is this where I can get the biggest bang for my buck? What will be the results of my investment? The dividends?
3. Why should I give now? With so many other worthy requests, how urgent is the cause?
4. Why me? Why are you coming to me? What's the reason I've been selected?

I rewrote the case to meet Mark's objections. He was right on target with many of his suggestions.

I returned with the new draft and Mark made one or two more suggestions. Suddenly the case became his. That's precisely what you want—donor buy in.

And Mark and Sheila, if you're wondering, did make a gift . . . for $1.5 million.

CHAPTER 9

"Next, in importance to books are their titles."
—Frank Crane

The Thread That Binds

In a moment, I'll share with you the best title I feel I ever penned. But first let me explain the vital purpose of the case statement's title.

The paramount role of your title is to whisk the reader into the first few paragraphs. It casts the theme and spirit. It's the melody you sing throughout.

The title must be sufficiently bold to capture the imagination and pique your readers' interest. It should enfold them in a dance of intrigue in which neither you nor they can escape the other's embrace.

You want to say to the reader: "Let me take you by the hand. There is something very special going on here. I want you to see for yourself. Come with me."

Every writer has a different method. I like coming up with a title early so I can use it as a theme throughout. There are other times when an engaging title eludes me.

When that happens, I write the piece, then review it to see what jumps out. Something always does. Like Edgar Allan Poe's purloined letter, it was always there, right in front of my eyes, just waiting for me to spot it. Then I go through the material and incorporate my title throughout, like a dominant colored thread selectively woven into the writing.

The concept for the title is a little like playing pinball. It may need a bit of careful jostling to light up. Then all of a sudden, a *coup de foudre*—a strike of lightning.

I prefer a title that's one or two words, three or four at the most. No semicolon, no subtitle.

If it's really appropriate (*really* being the operative word), use or adapt something you've seen before. Just so your readers haven't. You may want to change or invert a word or two. In the appendix, I've listed more than one hundred titles I've used. You're welcome to any of them.

I mentioned at the beginning of this chapter that I had a title I consider the most striking I've ever used. It was for the Chicago Missionary Society. I called it: FOR CHRIST'S SAKE!

The theme and feeling I was trying to convey, of course, were that everything the missionary society does is for the Kingdom. I wasn't unmindful, either, of the double meaning. I found that the Baptists felt it wicked, and the wicked felt it delightful.

CHAPTER 10

"To improve is to change; to be perfect is to change often."
—*Winston Churchill*

Determination, Direction, Dedication

I'm at a board meeting of a prominent organization in Omaha. They're speaking with me about a sizable campaign.

To gauge their readiness, I probe and ask a lot of questions. In the course of the discussion, the chairman boasts of their unwavering steadiness: "We've never changed our mission statement, not one word, in the eighty years of our existence."

I don't know very much about this organization, but I judge this campaign is in trouble from the start. The world has changed inside out in eighty years. Good grief, it's changed dramatically in the last twenty-four months.

This organization hasn't kept pace with the ever-ticking acceleration of change. If its mission statement is the same as it was eighty years ago, the parade has in all likelihood passed it by.

Fortunately, that's not your way. Your organization reviews its mission statement every few years, realizing it provides the road map, the signposts for your organization's existence and performance.

Flaubert could have been referring to a mission statement when he said, "It's the main dish of existence."

Keeping your mission current is essential. We've done studies, and the single most significant reason major donors say they give is because they believe in the organization's mission. Nothing else comes even a close second.

With that in mind, what I'm about to say might surprise you: you may wish to include your mission statement in your case, but it's not necessary.

What? Not include the mission statement?

Sure, somewhere in the case you need a description of your institutional objectives. These are the imperatives that propel you, the priorities that define you. You need to indicate how these objectives are unlike those of any other organization. And no group does its work as effectively as yours. This is what makes you fundable.

But if your mission statement is dull or difficult to understand or, worse still, outdated, consider paraphrasing it. Use only inspiring snippets in your case statement. You'll violate no sacraments.

My personal preference is to put both the history and the mission near the end, right before the dramatic close.

And keep it simple. Remember Peter Drucker's admonition about any mission statement: It should fit on a T-shirt and be easily understandable to a sixth grader.

CHAPTER 11

"Statistics do not convey emotion. They shock us for a minute or two, and then we click again."

—Madeleine Kunin

Statistics and Damn Lies

Even nineteenth-century British prime minister Benjamin Disraeli had something to say on the subject. "There are three kinds of lies," he proclaimed. "There are lies, damned lies, and statistics."

I'm careful in my case statements about statistics. I much prefer inspiring and convincing anecdotes. Statistics have all the spontaneity and passion of drying paint.

The typical reader doesn't have the time or patience to slog his or her way through a sludge of stats. But you'll find he or she is open to anecdotes. They provide action and feeling and more dramatically reveal your organization.

I'll give you an example.

> "It's late. I turn off the lights in my office and begin walking to the parking lot. I'm crossing the quadrangle when I feel a hand on my arm. It's one of our students. It's obvious she wants to talk.
>
> "First, let me tell you about Helen. It's one of the most extraordinary stories we've had at the college. When Helen first came to us as a student. . . ."

Something like that is so much more striking than saying, "A third of our student body is on some type of financial assistance."

Think in terms of the pelican.

You could write about "the odious British Petroleum spill off the coast of Louisiana. The worst ever. Over 680 million gallons of oil." But it's impossible to comprehend that much oil. And it certainly doesn't make the heart race.

Try this instead: "On the shore you can see pelicans—thousands of them. A rescuer is feverishly working on one whose wings are stuck like glue. Solvent can't undo the damage.

"When the rescuer tries to open the pelican's beautiful long beak, he finds it stuck, too. He knows he's going to lose this majestic bird. He's working against time. The death will be slow and painful. But inevitable."

That's a lot more concrete and descriptive than recording that an estimated 3,000 pelicans were killed as a result of the oil spill.

Here's another example. Let's say your student body has increased dramatically over the last ten years, or your membership has skyrocketed 15 percent every year for the last five, or your admissions to the emergency room have grown exponentially in the last three years. All of these facts lend themselves effectively to statistics and a graph.

If your statistics are impressive, by all means you should use them. It's what Walter Carpenter, former CEO of DuPont, referred to as "the eloquence of facts." But use them as a drunk might use a lamppost. Only for support, not illumination.

Long rows of statistics will make an actuary or accountant weep with joy. But for most readers, the eyes glaze over. Instead of the drudge of numbers, use graphs. They tell the story with impact and in a flash.

Here's where to consider statistics:

When showing your program is relevant. The need for your proposed program must be relevant. Donors look for that. The case you build and substantiate must be faultless and impregnable. To demonstrate relevancy, you need facts, details, and backup information. This is where statistics lend a helping hand.

> "At St. Mary's, we treat patients day and night. Every day. Every hour. Every minute. Last year, 128,000 people used our emergency room.
>
> "There isn't another hospital within 60 miles. The flow through our emergency room is unending. It's impossible to calculate how many would not make it through the night if it weren't for St. Mary's."

You can't fake relevancy. That would be like what former Texas governor Ann Richards described as "putting lipstick on a pig and calling her Monique."

When demonstrating the drama of your program. The case for your program must have dramatic and emotional appeal. It has to sizzle.

Statistics won't really help in adding drama, but at times they do open the door a crack for you. The great film director Fellini said, "Sometimes if you pull a little tail, you will find an elephant at the other end."

Use statistics when you want evidence of impressive growth. When you are looking, for instance, at the growth of an institution's membership over a ten-year period.

One way of showing statistics would be:

2004	6,703 members
2005	6,911 members
2006	6,107 members
2007	6,804 members
2008	7,407 members
2009	8,104 members
2010	8,906 members
2011	9,443 members
2012	10,001 members
2013	10,748 members
2014	11,217 members

Or, use a graph with a caption: Our Membership Has Grown Dramatically Over the Past Ten Years

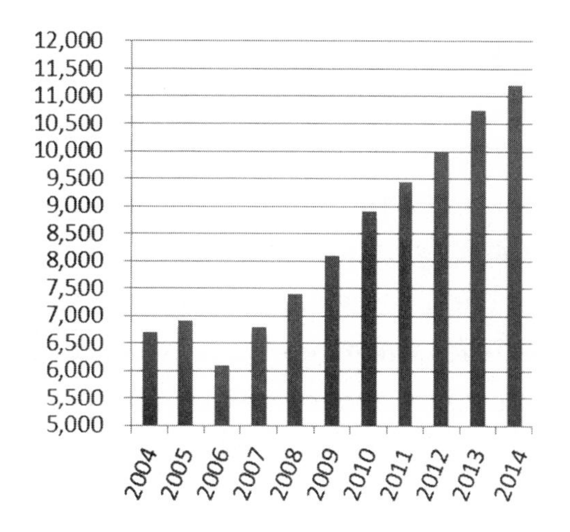

We conducted a campaign in Evanston, Illinois, for the Mental Health Association. We wondered how we could demonstrate in a striking way that one in six people have emotional issues, without using dozens of sentences and paragraphs.

We hit upon a simple solution. Our designer drew five stick figures with hands joined in a circle. One figure was off to the side. The caption read, "One out of six in our community needs your help."

When demonstrating urgency. There's nothing more critical to the success of your program than describing the urgency for the funds. "If we don't have the funds now, hundreds of abused and battered women will have nowhere to turn . . . ." As the great German philosopher Martin Heidegger wrote, "Urgency is the source of everything." Substantiating urgency is one place where statistics can be a welcome friend. The increase in the number of people served. Admissions to the emergency room. The number of homeless on the streets.

Your job is to convey the gravity of the situation—to make the situation dire. "It is February and frigid weather has struck. If we don't have the funds now, there will be 900 people on our streets tonight without dinner or shelter. More than 350 of them are children."

But tread lightly. If you present a barrage of statistics, they can have all the drama of a diva in decline. Whereas used judiciously to prove a point, stats can strip the flesh bare.

CHAPTER 12

"There is nothing like a dream
to create the future."
—Victor Hugo

Think in the Future

"That you're sitting before me in this church," the minister said, "is fact. That I am speaking from this pulpit is fact. That I believe anyone is listening is an act of faith."

Please have faith in what I'm about to tell you. I consider it gospel. Unless you're cheese or fine wine, age isn't important.

I bring this up simply to stress that in most instances, it's a mistake to start your case with your organization's history. Prospective investors are far more concerned with your dreams and vision for the future.

That's why I suggested earlier placing your history toward the end. I call that section of the case Waving the Flag. That's where I also include the mission—unabridged if it's really good, paraphrased if necessary to make it dramatic and understandable.

Instead of leading with history and the founding, I prefer beginning along these lines:

> We have been serving the homeless for fifty years. Uninterrupted. Around the clock. Every day. And on Thanksgiving and Christmas. Especially on Thanksgiving and Christmas.
>
> We extend hand and heart to all who enter. They find here a loving heart, a hearty meal, a clean and comfortable bed. Counseling when they're ready, chapel if they want it, and work opportunities. And all the coffee they can drink!
>
> They come to us. They come by the hundreds. Discouraged, distressed, weak in spirit. And yes, often on drugs. They leave changed. Some are changed forever.
>
> We are proud of our distinguished past. Because of our special approach, we are one of the premier institutions of our kind in the nation. We have established in this community an extraordinary record of service, unrelenting in our commitment and dedication to the homeless and this community.
>
> But it is to the future we look for our greatest achievements. What we envision is beyond

> anything of the past. That is why this program is so important to you . . . .

You see what I've done. I've tried to wrap the history and mission into describing the value of the projected program. Now, let me give you an example of the worst kind of history.

> "Our organization was founded in 1887 in Evansville, Indiana, in the old Trinity Lutheran Church on Center and Main Streets. A meeting was held in the sanctuary. Josiah Hockmeyer gathered eleven other kindred Lutherans to talk about the problems of . . . ."

This lesson in history is of interest only to the Hockmeyer family—and probably not all of them. It's as riveting as drywall. We'll never get the reader past the first paragraph.

I think of Dorothy Parker's review of a book: "This writing should not be tossed lightly aside but should be hurled with great force."

You want to honor the past, of course. But your real task, as far as your donors are concerned, is to transform your organization's history into a great tomorrow of incalculable service. You are an agent of transformation. You think endlessly in the future tense.

There is one important exception I want to note. If you have an uncommon and distinguished history, then certainly it deserves space in your opening paragraphs.

We managed the campaign for the Hermitage, President Andrew Jackson's home. It's located on a beautiful site outside of Nashville and was a working farm in Jackson's day.

When you visit the Hermitage, you drive on a narrow road leading to the property, up a long lane lined with two-hundred-year-old oak trees. There are cows and sheep and horses in the paddock. The sheds, the barns, all other structures have been restored just as they once were.

Quite suddenly, you're back in the 1830s. I wanted the reader to relive that momentous era. Here's what I wrote:

> Let me take you by the hand for a moment. Notice the tree-covered rolling hills and grass greener than you have ever seen. Spring is the best time of year at the Hermitage. Look at the burst of color. Apple and cherry blossoms everywhere. Come inside. This is the President's home, precisely like it was when he built it and lived here. He was a popular president. Even when he left office, dignitaries from all over

> the world still came to visit him. They came to this very Sitting Room where you are now. Walk with me into the parlor. Take a look. There's Jackson's favorite chair. And sitting next to him is his beloved wife. Did I tell you how he fought a duel and killed a man who made unkind remarks about Rachel? And look over there. That grandfather's clock is the very same one that was in that corner when the Jacksons lived here. It belonged to his father.

What I attempted was to get you into the president's home, sitting next to him and Rachel. That's what we did in the case.

If you have an institution with the kind of history of the Hermitage, you should use it, exploit it, and celebrate it. But don't make it a history lesson. Take the reader by the hand for a guided tour.

History in many cases doesn't entice or motivate. The typical reader doesn't have the patience to go slowly along, step by step, with the writing.

Your charge is to bond readers to the organization's new and dynamic vision.

They have joined you on a Harrison Ford-like quest for the Holy Grail. They're willing to chart new courses and shape new approaches. Your job is to make the organization edgy. Dissatisfied with the status quo. Willing to make the leap. Answer the call.

You sell the dream.

And if the dream doesn't frighten you a bit, you haven't been bold enough. You are the vision merchant. There is nowhere for the reader to hide.

CHAPTER 13

"Hell, there are no rules here—we're trying to accomplish something."
—*Thomas A. Edison*

Risk the Hoary No-Nos

For years, we've all learned the important lessons of grammar. William Strunk's *The Elements of Style* was our catechism, *The Chicago Manual of Style* our road map.

These and other guidebooks have a purpose. But as William Butler Yates said, Writing is blood, imagination, and inspiration come alive.

So forgive me for encouraging you to slip free from the surly bonds.

As far as your case statement is concerned, there is one overriding objective: that it be read. Nothing else matters.

With that in mind, I'm going to share with you some hard-won tips to help you tell your story.

1. It's perfectly acceptable to end your sentence with a preposition. There are some sentences that become awkward if you try to avoid what Miss Breckenridge in freshman English told you mustn't be done.

   Henry Watson Fowler wrote what many still consider the definitive volume, *A Dictionary of Modern English Usage*. This authority and language guru wrote "Prepositions are perfectly good words to end a sentence with."
2. It's acceptable to occasionally split infinitives (as I just did). Some of the best writers do. It often improves the flow.
3. By all means, feel you can begin a sentence with *And* or *But*. And you can even start a paragraph with either of these words.
4. One-sentence paragraphs are allowed. There are times when just a one-word paragraph is perfect.

   Really!
5. Contractions are permissible, at times encouraged. It's all right to do that. But not when you are trying to make a key point. Then it is not right.
6. It's not important what you put in. It's important what you leave out. "The test of good writing," Hemingway said, "is how much good stuff you leave out."

7. Write as if you're sending a note to your favorite aunt and the mechanic who works on her car.
8. Review your copy to see if you can expunge the word "that." In an earlier chapter, I first wrote: "Flaubert said that he wanted the writing to be so exciting that you could . . . ." When I revised the sentence, I deleted the two *thats*. Note how much stronger it is: "Flaubert said he wanted the writing to be so exciting you could . . . ."
9. Avoid jargon and be careful with initials and acronyms. You understand them, but your readers may not.
10. Use the present tense as much as possible. There's vitality and zest in the present.
11. Whatever its length, a stirring case should seem short. The reader wants it to go on forever like a Bach cantata. A dull piece, no matter how short, is too long.

    "How long should a case be?"As long as it needs to be. Not a word longer or shorter.
12. Expunge the word *excellence.* It's so overused it should be confined to naming goldfish. If you use it twice on a page, your hard drive will crash.
13. Make your verbs sweat. They add zing and zest. Let the verb do the work for you. Here's an example.

You could write, "Make certain your writing has power." Or, instead, "Writing that ignites."

14. Is it who? Or whom? Admit it. You have trouble with this like I do. I confess only because I know you understand. You can often eliminate that vexing decision by dropping the pesky word. Is it "That's the person with whom I'm having dinner"? Or "That's the person who I'm having dinner with"? Or write it as you would likely say it, and leave out the offending word: "That's the person I'm having dinner with."
15. Be discriminating with exclamation marks! The more you use them, the less BANG you get! Don't forget it! And if you feel you must use an exclamation mark, never use two!!
16. I try to avoid "etc." It's a matter of personal preference and style. But even Fowler (*Modern English Usage*) agrees: "To resort to using etc. is amateurish, slovenly, and incongruous." That's a bit strong, but you get the point.
17. Avoid the semicolon; it interrupts the flow and quashes momentum. Instead break your words into two short declarative sentences. That's what has force.
18. If possible, avoid a laundry list of items. It's what Nobel Laureate Patrick White called "too many

alternatives and no choices." If it's a long list, consider putting it in the appendix of your case.

19. After you've finished your first draft, read the material out loud. If it sounds like writing, rewrite it. Don't let pretty words (what Elmore Leonard calls "hoopdedoodle") get in the way of what you want to say.
20. Tell stories. You could write about a program this way:

"Last year, we had over 125,000 patients in our Emergency Room. We provide careful care to all."

Or this:

"Let me tell you about Julia. When the ambulance brought her to the emergency room, all she could move were her eyes. Twelve years old. Hit and run. She was rushed into our examining room. A team of our doctors . . . ."

21. Italics are *more difficult to read* than a regular font.
22. Reverse printing is pretty, in a limited way with headlines and pull-quotes, but it's more difficult to read.

23. A SENTENCE OR A PARAGRAPH OR EVEN A TITLE OF ALL CAPITAL LETTERS IS DIFFICULT TO READ.

24. Use adverbs with great care. Make the noun do the work. Ben Bradley, the great editor of the *Washington Post*, once told a new reporter, "If you ever decide to use an adverb, before you do—several days in advance—make an appointment with my secretary and come up to the third floor to see me to ask for permission."

25. Use connective words and phrases between paragraphs—such as *therefore, so you see, here's how.*

So you see if you do that, you keep the reader's attention from the last paragraph to the next.

26. I prefer paragraphs with no more than three sentences, four at the most. You've probably gathered that already from reading this book.

At the same time, vary the length of your paragraphs. No matter how inspirational the writing, if the paragraphs are mostly all the same length, it becomes boring.

27. Consider run-on and complex sentences as treasonous to your writing and your reader. Use short sentences. Pretend you're being paid by the period. And of course vary the number of words in your sentences. This variation adds spice.

28. I try to use words with no more than three syllables. If the reader cracks a tooth on a polysyllabic—I mean, hard—word, it's tough to swallow the writing that follows.

Take a lesson from Lincoln's powerful second inaugural address. No one with a pulse can read it without awe. "Fondly do we hope, fervently do we pray, that this mighty scourge of war may pass away . . . . With malice toward none, with charity for all." And the most eloquent of all, only four single-syllable words long: "And the war came."

It was a marvel of economy with only 701 words. There were 505 words of one syllable and 122 of two syllables.

29. Fondle your words. When you review your first draft, caress each word to determine if it's the best one. Or perhaps there's another that's more descriptive.

30. Beware of overdoing the flamboyant and spark. It's what Gertrude Stein referred to as too much much. An overabundance of electricity in your writing will make your reader's hair frizzy.

31. Write as clearly and unadornedly as possible. "Write in plain English. Use words everyone can understand," said Hemingway. In poetry and fiction, there may be a place for ambiguity, but never in a case statement.

32. Instead of using bullets (•), number your items. A listing with numbers stands out and is read. Bullets are dull and listless—much as Miss Breckenridge's afternoon class on a warm spring day.

33. Make effective and frequent use of headings and subheadings. They add punch and give the reader a necessary breather. Too much copy without a break can cause reader-indigestion. Readers graze the material before they sit down for a full meal of reading.

34. Be scrupulous. Check for typos, misspellings, missing words, and columns of figures that don't add up. (Some accountant or engineer is certain to check your addition.)

Get caught on even the most modest infraction, and the reader will challenge your entire document (it'll likely be your largest potential donor whose name you misspelled).

Imagine what havoc it must have caused among the bishops and priests (and the absolute glee and abandonment among parishioners) to come across the Seventh Commandment in the new edition of the Bible especially prepared for King Charles I. It read, "Thou shall commit adultery."

35. Use photographs throughout. One to a page isn't too many. They must be compelling and tell a story, and they should supplement, not detract, from the text.

    All photographs should have captions. *Caption* and *captivating* have the same root. Can you imagine a photograph in any magazine that doesn't have an interpretive and identifying caption?

    Small photographs lack drama and emotional appeal. Those who test this sort of thing tell me that one or two people in a photograph is more alluring and intriguing than a group shot.

36. While your job is to write the case, you should also have a role in approving the design. Alan Peckolich is one of the nation's great designers. He tells me that a design can lie on a page like a plate of liver. Or it can sing and dance. Your role is to link arms—your rousing copy with the designer's awe-inspiring layout—in a perpetual samba.

37. There's an old adage about writing. Write fast. Edit slow. I'll tell you what I like to do. I stay away from my draft a day or two. I let it steep, like a

good pot of tea. I find I can get back to it with a fresh outlook.

38. The nicest thing a reader can say about your case is "You make me feel I'm right there with you."

39. This one I purloined from Mark Twain: "Substitute 'damn' every time you're inclined to write 'very'; your editor will delete it and the writing will be just as it should be."

CHAPTER 14

"When asked, 'How do you write?' I invariably answer, 'one word at a time.'"

—Stephen King

Getting Ready

It was Ernest Hemingway who said, "The story I'm writing exists. I know that. It's written in perfect fashion. It is someplace, somewhere in the air. All I need do is prepare. Then I'll find my story and simply copy it."

The same can be said for you. To begin, you need to prepare.

That means having on hand the items I'm about to list. At first, you'll feel you don't need all of them. But I can attest from decades of experience and thousands of cases that you do.

- A brief history of your organization.
- Your mission statement.

- Your organization's short- and long-range objectives and goals.
- Your marketing or program plans to reach these objectives and goals.
- The results of a recent market research study, if available.
- The annual budget of your organization, including a breakdown of your sources of support (corporate contributions, individual contributions, foundation grants, United Way revenue if you're a member agency, and fees).
- A description of your major programs and the rationale of how and why they meet specific client needs.
- Membership or client information, including how many participate in your programs and the total number you serve. Also, information on membership or client demographics.
- Information on the giving sources within the community or your constituencies. Include the sources you'll target for the campaign or ongoing fundraising. Any relevant research about your donors is particularly helpful here.
- Information on urgent community needs your organization will address in the next few years. Statistics to support these claims help define the areas of need.

- Within the context of your organization's mission, how will you strive to meet emerging needs? It's most effective to cite specific programs or initiatives and specific participation goals. Emphasize the urgency.
- Specifics on your fundraising program, including the total goal and the cost of any individual projects.
- Information on the role of the campaign and how the funds will translate into the people served and lives changed and saved.
- Endorsements from institutional leaders, recognized community or constituent leaders, and appropriate government officials, to give life to the material and help build a persuasive case.
- Any aspect of your programming, history, or individual relationships your organization holds dear. They elevate the campaign's importance.
- The biography of the founders, the CEO, and leaders who are key to your organization's vitality. These items provide another human element. But when you write, go light on the history and the founders. That's not your future.
- Interviews with the board chair, one or two board members, the CEO, any other appropriate staff, and several interviews with clients participating in programs you've identified as instrumental to

the campaign. Also include influential men and women in your community or in your constituency whose voices carry weight. And one or two major donors.
- Photographs of your facility, staff, and clients working together, clients being served, and shots of individuals to be interviewed. These help generate empathy for your cause.

In appendix D, I've included a much more complete list you should review.

One last thing: Organize all of your material before you begin writing. If you don't, you'll be constantly shuffling and sifting piles of paper.

"I must carefully prepare," said Norman Mailer. "If I don't, I spend my time thinking about what I should have for dinner. Then I make myself another drink."

You're now ready to begin.

CHAPTER 15

"I begin with the first sentence and trust to Almighty God for the second."
—*Eudora Welty*

You Simply Begin

I've never hiked Everest or its neighbor K2, but writing strikes me as similar to climbing a mountain with a rock face like glass. You find only a few crevice handles to hang onto desperately.

E.B. White knew a thing or two about putting off the start of his writing. "I rise in the morning torn between the desire to improve the world . . . and the desire to enjoy the world. This makes it hard to plan the day for my writing."

Unfortunately, you never find the time to write. You have to make the time.

Each writer has a style uniquely his or her own. I'm going to suggest some strategies that are helpful to me.

They may help you create your case with a sense of force and urgency.

First, don't lean over backwards to present your facts too objectively. Sure, tell the truth. But state your case in a manner that propels readers to reach for their checkbooks. Make your organization look as if it's been destined since the beginning of time to address this special challenge at this very moment in history. It's what poet Mark Tupper said was "A call from God to waken men."

Second, studies show that most gifts, especially larger ones, are made viscerally, not cerebrally. So appeal first to the emotions and then to the intellect. That means personalizing statistics with true stories and case studies. Think *exclamation* rather than *explanation*.

Write about a specific heart patient or a girl who was able to continue her education only because of the scholarship she received. Tell about Brianna, a child born with cerebral palsy who takes her first step. Use the dramatic story about Addison, a delinquent whose life was turned around by the Boys Club.

Speak about real men and women. Young people whose lives you've touched. They are the composers of your music. Be specific, use names. If it makes the reader tingle and break out in goosebumps . . . well, you're on your way to a gift!

Third, make your words inch-perfect. When you're talking about your project, say what miracles it makes possible (present tense—not would make possible or will make possible).

Fourth, don't ask for help. Instead, talk in terms of the opportunity the program offers the donor. Write about the important investment he or she can make and how huge the dividends are.

Fifth, let your probable donors know of the amazing results their gifts make possible. Make them feel it couldn't be done without them. I use the BOY rule when I write—Because Of You.

It's not about your organization. It's not even about money. It's about changing and saving lives. Don't ask for their help. Ask for their hearts.

Sixth, be brief about expressing any problems. Devote more time to the opportunities at hand. Donors want to hear the good news, positive outcomes, and results that count.

Focus on the incredible work being accomplished in a less-than-adequate facility. That's better than describing a place so squalid and unsafe that the organization couldn't possibly be doing a decent job.

Seventh, tell readers what you want them to do. Move them to action. If the case is sufficiently dramatic and appealing, it transforms the institution into a cause and the cause into a crusade. And crusades are what motivate men and women to action.

"Thinking is the activity I love best," Isaac Asimov said, "and writing is simply thinking through my fingers. I can write up to eighteen hours a day. I've done better than fifty pages a day. Nothing interferes with my concentration. You could put on an orgy and I wouldn't even look up—well maybe once."

CHAPTER 16

"Those who write clearly have readers, those who write obscurely have commentators."

—Albert Camus

Leave Nothing Unanswered

John Middleton Murray says that a truly great piece of writing is an exciting tale to the simple, a parable to the wise, and a direct revelation of passionate wonder to the man who's made it part of his being.

No one said it would be easy. A clean sheet of paper or a blank screen waits, daring you for an irresistible script.

Earlier, I described the eight elements of a case. I put them in a particular order, but don't be unduly concerned about how they fall into place. There are times when it's much more compelling to start with the vision or the urgency. And sometimes, historical facts or details about current services can be handled best as exhibits in an appendix. You needn't follow a rigid guide. You're a dream merchant. Write with conviction and zeal and find your own rhythm.

What counts is that you leave nothing unanswered or open to challenge. And yes, one thing more. You end up with a case that represents your organization with style, grace, and integrity. You want a *can't put down, can't turn down* piece.

For years I've looked for an instrument of some sort to help me assess the writing of some of our staff. And one that helps clients evaluate material they've written.

I felt that what was needed was a tool to help examine and grade a case. Since I never found such an instrument, I developed one of my own.

I think you're going to like it. You can challenge me on some of the items, but I do feel a bit like Alfred Austin, English poet laureate at the turn of the last century. He referred to celestial inspiration in all he did. "I dare not alter anything I do. It all comes to me from above."

Go to appendix E. Use the *CasE*valuator to rate the twelve essential factors that determine the effectiveness of a successful case. Indicate the points for each item in the right-hand column. Total the points to score your case.

CHAPTER 17

"A goal properly set is halfway reached."
—*Zig Ziglar*

The End of the Beginning

A shepherd persuades his sheep that their interests and his are the same. In writing a case, you are the shepherd.

Keep that in mind. Your most significant job is to motivate your reader to make an investment in your great cause. You make it irresistible.

Whatever else you cover in your case, your job is to have the reader live in great anticipation of providing a gift that will make a consequential difference.

When Christ approached a leper, he didn't say, "We haven't been having a great deal of success with leprosy lately. But if you follow my advice, you'll have a decent shot of survival over the next five years."

No, what He said was, "You are healed."

That's how emphatic and unmistakably unequivocal you need to be with your case. Resolute.

You've finished your draft. You've read it out loud (that's something you definitely want to do). If some words are hard to pronounce, readers will stumble over them. Also, you're listening to the rhythm.

Now, go over it one more time. Your objective is to move the reader to action. You make certain it doesn't read like a press release. This is a personal message "from me to you."

Finally, keep in mind the major reasons people will give to your organization. In the canons of fundraising, these nine are ripe for beatitude. Make certain you respond to them in your case.

1. They believe in the work of your organization and your unique qualification to provide the program and services you project.
2. They recognize the urgent need you describe and agree that yours is the most capable organization to address it.
3. Their gift will change lives or save lives.
4. They have the funds to make the gift.
5. They eschew status quo. They are change-agents. They want to invent the future.
6. They want to make a difference. They're not willing to creep when they feel the impulse to soar.

7. There is philanthropic intent. They understand the importance and the joy of giving.
8. They wish to join others in a worthy cause. To borrow a telling phrase from Harold Isaacs, "they feel the scratches on their heart."
9. You ask. You ask them to make an investment.

I am reminded of all you and I go through in preparing a case—the sturm and drang. But then I think of water lilies in a pond. They represent the finished product. The lilies burst with color and allure. But hidden beneath them lies a quagmire of roots and tendrils.

Think of your case like the unfolding of Scheherazade. The symphonic suite starts with energy. It then builds to an all-encompassing crescendo of excitement and emotion.

The music is yours. You are the hero of the composition.

CHAPTER 18

"When you're drowning you don't think, I would be incredibly pleased if someone would notice I'm drowning and come and rescue me. You just scream."

—John Lennon

A Committee Revises the Copy

"When I use a word," Humpty Dumpty said in a rather scornful tone, "it means just what I choose it to mean—neither more nor less." Lewis Carroll understood a thing or two about having a committee review a draft.

Writing a case is a strange experience. It involves passion and endurance, a rare combination of desire and grunt work. All this is often at odds with each other. You wonder what's more difficult—writing the case or protecting it against the committee that wants to revise it.

When a group is asked to review or edit a case, something mystifying takes place, kindling qualities that are somewhere between belligerence and sadism.

"No passion in the world," said H.G. Wells, "is equal to the passion to alter someone else's draft." There's something uncontrollably satisfying in reworking someone else's material.

It will happen. Count on it. You'll have to submit your captivating copy to a committee for review. That's because there's no great or small decision to which an organization will respond without a committee meeting.

Search all the parks
In all your cities—
You'll find no monuments
To any committees

If you have an easily bruised ego, writing may not be the right career choice. This is no place for sissies. The key to a happy life for a case writer is knowing how to deal with Plan B.

I can attest to the distress firsthand.

I remember vividly one case I presented to the committee of a major university. I thought the writing was consecrated, as irreproachable as the presentation of a menu by a French head waiter.

I pass out copies for the committee to read. I watch the chair as she turns the pages. Page one, page two. When she gets to page three, she has the expression of someone about to undergo a root canal.

"I don't like it!" she says.

I'm thinking of her as the Queen of Hearts in Alice in Wonderland. At any moment she's ready to shout, "Off with his head."

The man next to her chimes in. He doesn't like it either. Few things are more upsetting than getting a second opinion you don't like any better than the first.

Then someone else adds, "I don't want to be a devil's advocate, but . . . ." You know what's coming. A devil's advocate is the guy who rocks the boat and then persuades everyone else there's a storm at sea.

Like me, you want to scream, "Stop!" But instead you listen and nod. You might even find yourself agreeing. What I find is that if a committee doesn't feel excited and motivated by your precious copy, something may indeed be sorely wrong.

Keep in mind that the first draft is the down-draft. You get everything down. The second draft is the up-draft. You fix it up.

If it takes a third draft, chances are you're in serious trouble. Trying to patch it up at this point will be as difficult as reconstructing a spider web. You may want to start all over.

No one likes submitting work to a committee. But let's face it—that's almost certainly what's going to happen. Get ready for the pain.

Someone once asked Clarence DeMar, seven-time winner of the Boston Marathon, to expound on his racing philosophy. "Run like hell, and get the agony over with."

If you keep the following points in mind, it will help you have the strength and endurance to bear the wild ideas of others.

Attempt to keep the number critiquing your copy to as few as possible. I usually say to the board chair or the CEO something like this: "Let's keep the number reviewing the case small. If we have twenty looking at it, then we'll get twenty different opinions. Give it to three or four to read. Especially if they're your largest potential donors. If they like it, you know it's on target."

The objective of the case is to be read, dramatically inspire, and move the reader to action. If that doesn't happen with the people who review your copy—it may be your copy that's the problem. That's the sad truth of it. It can be like a pistol shot in the middle of a concert. It is blaring, upsetting, contemptible—but something you can't refuse to notice.

I like to let the group know (before they read the material or when I pass it out at a meeting) why I took the approach I did. "Let me explain why I chose the title I did. As I went through the material . . . ." Doing this helps preempt any issues or concerns the committee might have.

There are times when they can't tell you how they want you to improve it. It just doesn't do anything for them. They don't know what they want and won't be happy until they get it. If this is the case, you may have to go to Plan B. That could mean another entire rewriting. I usually press the committee to tell me what I need to do. "Do you not find it urgent? Does it not move you to action? Are there parts that are acceptable? Help me understand. If I don't I can't improve it." I keep pushing for answers.

You don't have to use every suggestion. If you have a lot of people reading the copy or a high number of suggestions, evaluate what's most important. Otherwise, you embrace a middle—and a muddle. The first rule of tinkering is to save the most important parts.

If anything can go wrong, it will. If anything can't go wrong, it still will. Begin the next draft. Perform a series of deep-breathing exercises. It will calm your nerves.

You wait for the decision. You feel like the nerve-tingling Roman gladiator. Is it thumbs up or thumbs down?

If it is thumbs down, think of Frank Sinatra's favorite

song. It becomes your hymn: "Every time I find myself flat on my face, I just pick myself up and get back in the race."

That's life.

Coda

Perhaps like me, you hate saying goodbye. It's so final. Someone said *gone* is the saddest word in the language. I agree.

That's why I didn't call this section an afterword, epilogue, or anything of the sort. Coda seems just right somehow: a passage that brings a movement or a composition to its closing. With a coda, you know there's more coming. At some point.

I thought of this book, in a modest way, like Tchaikovsky's 1812 Overture. Cannons roaring, bells clanging, cymbals smashing, the music soaring. While the book may not be so triple-forte for you, hopefully there is some inspiration and direction that will help.

Every book I write is like a first love for me. I was minding my own business before this book came along. Then I felt the urge. I was in love again. I feel like Primo Levi. "When the time came, I needed to write this book. I had a pathological need to do it."

Writing is not my profession. If someone asks me if I am a writer, I would say I am not. I am a fundraiser who happens to have the urge to scribble.

You have read the book and sense how strongly I feel on certain issues. Now do as Sherlock Holmes said to Watson: “You know my methods. Apply them.”

And, really, this book doesn’t end here. As it closes, it’s just a beginning. Coda.

APPENDIX

Questions I'm Most Often Asked about Case Statements

What is the major objective of a case statement?

I'll say it in three words: To be read. That seems obvious, but not all cases are easy to get through. And the reader has no tolerance for boredom. Really, the job of your case is to incite action. It has to be sufficiently inspiring and motivating to move the prospective donor from the mind to the heart to the checkbook. Sure, it needs to provide information, but it must be far more than that. It has to have majesty and boldness. In the simplest of terms, the case is your vision and dream with a dollar sign.

Who should write the case?

It can certainly be written by a member of your staff. Many organizations have powerful writers. The problem with a staff member is that it almost always takes longer. This doesn't have to happen if the writer is relieved of other responsibilities and can take three to four weeks to work on the case full-time.

Keep this in mind, too. The quality of the writing often depends on the affection the writer feels for the organization. It has to be a love affair. This is true for someone on your staff—even truer if you outsource the writing. There are times when one of our writers returns from an assignment with a ho-hum attitude. "How did it go?" I ask. "Oh, okay. They're doing a fine job." If the writer feels the organization is doing a so-so job, I know it's going to be a so-so case.

How long should the case be?

Recently I read in a professional journal that case statements should be no more than two or three pages long. The author said that busy prospects won't take the time to read more. I hear that, too, from board members. Forgive me, but that's nonsense! You can't sell a dream and a vision in two or three pages. A case should be as long as it needs to be. Not a sentence longer or a sentence shorter. Typically our cases run about twelve to fifteen pages. You can't possibly engage the reader, describe the need, create the urgency, make the case, and motivate the would-be donor to make a gift in just two or three pages.

What do readers look for?

Readers want to know why they should support your organization. Why this project? Why now? And why me? The case has to respond to these questions. People want to give to bold and exciting programs that make a difference. They want to create resounding change. They want results. But here's a warning: keep it as simple as possible. If you present the reader with more than three or four priorities, you're spreading yourself too thin. A famous attorney said that if you send the jury out for deliberation with six or seven things to remember, they don't remember anything.

What are the major elements that must be covered in a case?

It all begins with the title. You seek something that's compelling. Or surprising. Maybe even a little shocking. A good title will move readers to your first few paragraphs, which are crucial. If you lose readers here, you won't get them back. Next you begin explaining the need. You detail how your organization is unmatched in its ability to surmount the problem. "No other organization is as well prepared . . . ." And you convey urgency. "We cannot wait. We must move forward now."At some point, perhaps in the middle of your case, you need to describe your organization's mission. It's your guiding anchor. Finally there's the benediction. You bless all that's been written. You solemnize the marriage of the reader to the need.

Is the case only for a capital campaign?

Most think of a case that way. But it's every bit as important for annual giving. Men and women need to know why they should give to an ongoing or annual effort.

Will one case do the job for all constituents?

For years, I thought so. But what I realize now is that different constituents have different needs. And what appeals to one stakeholder may not interest another. Take for instance a university. Alumni are likely motivated differently than parents. Differently than faculty members. Differently from foundations. You get the idea. I believe you need to accommodate at least two or three of your primary constituencies. Plan a case for each. Seventy-five or eighty percent of the piece will be the same for all. But you'll tailor it appropriately for the needs and appeal for each specific constituency.

Is there a preferred writing style?

I find a conversational style makes it most readable. I tell our writers to prepare the material as if they were talking to their favorite aunt or the mechanic who services her car. I like using colloquial terms, short sentences, short paragraphs. Your document isn't meant for an English teacher. It's directed to the person you need to motivate to make a gift.

What's the best way to present the case?

I have a strong preference here. I like putting it in a three-ring binder. That's because no one ever throws away a three-ring binder. In my experience, a fancy brochure, four-color and blind embossed, isn't as likely to be read. I do something else you might consider. For major would-be donors, I mark the case with a big rubber stamp that says DRAFT. I seek their ideas and comments. As a matter of fact, I usually send it in advance of my visit (even providing a red pen so they can mark it up—and they do).

Does the case create donors?

I don't believe you can create donors. But you can certainly create passion and commitment among those who read your case. Those are the results you aim for and expect.

Sample Theme Lines

Here are themes I chose at random from cases we've written. Some may be a perfect match for a piece you're working on. You're welcome to use them.

I approve virtually every title before it's sent to the client for consideration. At the time, I thought each one was very near brilliant!

Renaissance by the Riverside
(Tampa Museum of Art)

To Grow, To Serve
(Salvation Army, Iowa)

The Skill to Heal, The Spirit to Care
(Florida Hospital Waterman)

Building the Future, Restoring the Past
(Dona Ana Arts Center)

A New Stage for a Grand Old Stage Coach
(Stage Coach Players)

Scholarship on Fire!
(Baptist Theological Seminary)

Waiting in the Wings
(South Bend Civic Theatre)

Lessons for Tomorrow
(Allegany College/Bedford Campus)

A Caring Legacy . . . A Bright Future
(Children's Shelter, Texas)

A Burning Issue, A Flame of Hope
(Old Firehouse Rescue Shelter)

Wilderness in the City
(Sand Creek Regional Greenway)

A Building to Treasure, A Treasury of Knowledge
(Franklin Public Library)

Exceeding Expectations
(Scott & White Medical Center)

Some Enchanted Evenings
(Center for the Performing Arts)

From Success to Significance
(Concordia University)

The Crossroads of Life
(Coffeyville Regional Medical Center)

Building on a Dream
(West Virginia Public Theatre)

"Something Holy"
(Mt. Tabor Center)

Everyone's Favorite Place
(West Monmouth County YMCA)

With God's Grace
(Los Altos Methodist)

An Unmatched Spirit
(East Texas Medical/Rusk)

Beyond Measure
(Children's Hospital Medical Center)

A Matter of Heart
(University Community Hospital)

Close to Our Heart
(Good Samaritan Community Healthcare)

A Promise of Renewal
(Providence St. Peter Hospital)

Hope for Tomorrow . . . Today
(Salvation Army, Lincoln)

Keeping Faith with the Future
(Atlantic General Hospital)

Time to Climb Another Peak
(Pikes Peak Region YMCA)

A Place for New Beginnings
(Family Services Davidson County)

Setting the Stage for Life
(Woodside High School Auditorium)

A Vision and A Reality
(North Valley Hospital)

A Tomorrow of Uncommon Promise
(Mississippi College)

Part of Your Life
(Carson Tahoe Hospital)

One Family at a Time
(Birmingham YMCA)

Building on the Best
(Mission Hospital)

Welcome Home
(Ohio Masonic Home)

Who Will Take Care of Us?
(Bryan School of Nursing)

When a House Becomes a Home
(FarmHouse Fraternity)

Saving the Last Great Places
(The Nature Conservancy)

The Head of Class
(Powhatan School)

Setting A New Stage
(Lawrence Community Theatre)

A Matter of Life
(Carondelet Foundation)

Depend On Us. For Life!
(Baptist Medical Center)

How Does Your Garden Grow?
(Quail Botanical Gardens)

Keeping A Covenant
(Kansas City YMCA)

Keeping Pace with Tomorrow
(Baylor Medical Center/Grapevine)

What's In A Namesake?
(Lincoln College)

The Right Thing to Do
(Queen of the Valley Hospital)

A Lifeline of Hope
(The Center for Prevention of Abuse)

We're Here for Life
(St. Mary's Hospital)

"Whenever There Is A Need . . ."
(St. Thomas Child & Family Center

Building on a Promise
(Indiana Chapter, Red Cross)

With God's Blessing
(Church of the Ascension)

Give A Girl A Future . . .
(Girls Inc. of Greater Santa Barbara)

That Time of Your Life
(Munroe Regional Medical Center)

Rekindling a Legacy of Care
(Door County Memorial Hospital)

The Campaign for Life
(Blodgett Butterworth Health Care Foundation)

A Woman's Place
(Riverview Hospital)

A Place Where Faith and Healing Meet
(Pastoral Care Programs)

Setting the Stage for a Dramatic Future
(Toledo Repertoire Theatre)

Dream On and Believe
(Oklahoma State University)

Beautiful Music. Forever
(Evansville Philharmonic Orchestra)

A Path With A Purpose
(MeritCare Health Systems)

Making Beautiful Music
(South Dakota Symphony)

Discover the River of Dreams
(Pocomoke River Discovery Center)

A Living Heritage of Humanity
(African American Cultural Center)

Summa Cum Laude
(Notre Dame)

How Do You Top A Miracle?
(Franklin Road Academy)

Just Imagine!
(Children's Museum for Mississippi)

Welcome to Our World
(Leesburg Regional Medical Center)

The Nature of Tomorrow
(Howell Wetlands)

More Than A Hospital
(Rice Memorial Hospital)

Tradition Meets the Challenge
(Camp Becket/Chimney Corners YMCA)

Once In Our Lifetime
(Sacred Heart Medical Center)

It's Life That Matters
(East Texas Medical Center)

Vision Inspired
(Trust for Public Land)

Making Miracles Every Day
(Children's Museum)

Places Never Before Gone
(Saint Alphonsus Medical Center)

A Covenant with Tomorrow
(Scripps Hospital)

Grabbing the Reader

What follows is a random sampling of some opening and closing paragraphs from our case statements. My hope is that some will inspire you to even greater heights when creating your case.

Opening Paragraph

At this very moment, an invisible epidemic is sweeping across this country. Last year it claimed 170,000 lives, and the number keeps rising. Right now, it's the fourth leading cause of death by disease in the United States. Nearly sixteen million Americans have this disease, and a third of them don't even know it. It isn't cancer. It isn't AIDS, or Alzheimer's. This invisible epidemic is diabetes.

American Diabetes Association

Opening Paragraphs

There are outstanding universities in the world. Few are truly great. Some excel in particular areas of learning. But none, not one, can compare with Oxford's overall achievements and ranking in all aspects of its endeavors.

Some would insist we are the most outstanding University in the world. Most would certainly say we are among that small, select group of the greatest.

And now we undertake this bold campaign. We shall secure a future every bit as great as our past. Greater still. We shall strengthen our community of scholars in important ways that ensure our leadership in the pantheon of the world's higher education.

The University of Oxford

Closing Paragraphs

Who now walks these hallowed halls to become tomorrow's Prime Ministers, great academicians and scientists, Nobel laureates?

We educate the world, the new century's gifted men and women. This is our commitment. Our graduates will find the cures, lead governments, direct corporations, guide faculties, and solve some of the world's most puzzling dilemmas.

This is our destiny.

The University of Oxford

Opening Paragraph

The achievements of Roanoke College's last decade owe a great debt to the sacrifice and struggle of all Roanoke generations. It has been a long journey from 1842 to today. But, every new student or tenured professor or brick or book is a step into the future, and an advance toward the victory of significant distinction.

Roanoke College
Roanoke, Virginia

Closing Paragraph

We believe in the creation of inspired lives produced by the miracle of hard work. We are not frightened by the challenges of reality, but believe that we can change our conception of this world and our place within it. So we work, plan, build, and dream. We believe that one must earn the right to dream. Our talent, discipline, and integrity will be our contribution to a new world. Because we believe we can take this place, this time, and this people—and make a better place, a better time, and a better people. With God's help, we will either find a way, or make one.

Providence-St. Mel
Chicago, Illinois

Opening Paragraph

Lakeside School is a place where bright, eager, energetic and motivated students and teachers work together to do amazing things in and out of the classroom.

Whether working with DNA samples in the lab, hiking the beaches of the Washington Coast, or playing a LaCrosse match on the field, Lakeside Faculty and students share an enthusiasm and a love of learning.

Lakeside School
Seattle, Washington

Opening Paragraph

For 150 years, the YMCA has been a pioneering force in the United States—a force so powerful that, as we begin the 21st Century, it is the most successful social institution this country has ever known. Above all, the YMCA is about people—all ages, races, religions and incomes.

YMCA of the USA

Closing Paragraph

Students shall find wisdom here and faith. In steel and stone, in character and thought, they shall find beauty, adventure, and moments of high victory.

The University of Pittsburgh
Pittsburgh, Pennsylvania

Opening Paragraph

It was a different world when Orange County State College was established on 225 acres of orange groves in 1957. It is an even more dramatically different world today as the College of Business and Economics of California State University, Fullerton looks to a tomorrow that is already here.

Orange County State College
Fullerton, California

Opening Paragraph

Be it known by all who enter our doors that Christ is the reason for this school. He is the unseen but ever present teacher in its classes. He is the model of its faculty and the inspiration of its students.

The Summit Country Day School
Cincinnati, Ohio

Opening Paragraph

Time does not stand still. Ever. It takes away and marches on. So must a great university. Success breeds confidence. We cannot and will not rest on our laurels. There is much more to accomplish.

Oklahoma State University
Oklahoma City, Oklahoma

Closing Paragraph

Our mission and values call us to be first and foremost a ministry of healing. We can't be viewed by ourselves or others as just another healthcare business. It's simply not who we are. We are all on a personal journey of faith.

Saint Thomas Health Services
Nashville, Tennessee

Opening Paragraph

The moment has come for Pepperdine to launch into a new era. Each year our journey will be attended by fresh adventures . . . our sails have caught the winds of change—and in assurance and anticipation, the voyage begins.

Pepperdine University
Malibu, California

Opening Paragraph

If you could invest $100 and get $716 in return, would you? The question is real, because you earn seven times what you give when you invest in the early months and years of a child's life.

United Way of America

Opening Paragraph

While higher education experiences a rattling of its moral foundations, Brigham Young University stands firm. It holds fast to its founding commitment to integrate spiritual and secular knowledge. As we press forward with this historic campaign for Brigham Young University, we recognize that BYU has yet to achieve its great potential.

Brigham Young University
Provo, Utah

Closing Paragraph

But it is our students to whom we have the most urgent responsibility. Although our future will soon be in their hands, their preparation for the future is now in ours. To them we will entrust the reins of government, the management of our businesses, the education of future generations of our children, and the leadership of our global society.

What they are taught, and how they are taught, is of infinite importance.

The ultimate success of this effort depends on you. Your support will indeed help light the way. Now is the time to increase support of this great school. It is time to press forward, a time to celebrate, a time to shine.

Brigham Young University
Provo, Utah

Opening Paragraphs

There are no hum-drum days at Highland Hospital. There is nothing commonplace about the work that goes on there. What would be considered exceptional in some other hospitals is the typical and ordinary here. That's the wonder of it all: That within the walls of an aging, inner-city healthcare facility—amazing people are doing heroic things with enormous pride and dedication, to deliver extraordinary care to the sickest and most marginalized people in Alameda County.

The stories that unfold at Highland are both brave and brutal, horrendous and heartwarming. They bear witness to human tragedy on a huge scale and to human caring on an even grander scale. They carry messages of hope, caring, and commitment.

Highland Hospital
Alameda County Medical Center
Oakland, California

Opening Paragraphs

There is little doubt that the new century presents challenging times for higher education, and especially for independent higher education. But with challenge comes opportunity. Since 1870, Wilmington College has combined the practical and liberal arts to help students make a living and make a life. The Wilmington experience continues to have a transforming influence on student's lives.

Our Quaker heritage places peace, nonviolence and social justice at the heart of the College's mission. These values shape what we do and inform who we are.

Wilmington College
Wilmington, Ohio

Opening Paragraph

World Christian Broadcasting invites you to join its band of realistic dreamers, who have learned how to turn an impossible mission into one of history's greatest success stories.

World Christian Broadcasting
Franklin, Tennessee

Opening Paragraphs

We welcome the critically ill with hope, and the healthy with a promise of an even brighter future. Once entering the doors, the patient is never, from that day forward, a stranger again.

If we are to defeat the big killers—heart disease and cancer—we must strive for no less than being one of the top medical centers in the country. This requires total commitment. We are prepared and poised. We can provide a Pathway to Life.

New life. Our dream is eradicating cancer and eliminating heart disease. Until we achieve our dream, there is no rest.

Spectrum Health
Grand Rapids, Michigan

Opening Paragraph

There's no such thing as a typical day at the Museum of Discovery and Science. There's nothing commonplace about the learning that goes on here. What would be considered exceptions in many schools is simply an ordinary day here. That's the wonder of it all: That within the walls of a facility that now serves twice the number of people it was built for, dedicated staff members are doing extraordinary things and igniting in all who walk through its doors a newfound curiosity and passion for learning about the world around them.

Museum of Discovery and Science
Ft. Lauderdale, Florida

Opening Paragraph

Every day we are reminded that we are building a university that will last long beyond the days that our individual footsteps mark these paths. Indeed, we are building an institution of higher education that, as with all great universities, is designed to serve not just the moment, but the ages.

Chapman University
Orange, California

Closing Paragraph

There is no limit to what a dedicated group of people can accomplish when they are led with respect, joined as a team, and focused on a dream. The Campaign for Change is a revolution. A war. The transformation of a community and the building of better futures for its children. Economic, academic, family and racial barriers to achieving this transformation must come down.

The Urban League
Broward County, Florida

Opening Paragraph

At Drew, a historic stone gateway opens onto a University with a vision for tomorrow. A place of innovation and interaction, Drew has prospered over its relatively short history. Small, selective and passionate, Drew is teaching the liberal arts within the context of today. Given this mission and its superb location, Drew offers students one of the most stimulating environments for learning and research—for discovery—in higher education. Against this background, we have launched a campaign to raise $62 million to build new gateways to and from the world.

Drew University
Madison, New Jersey

Opening Paragraph

Approaching its fourth century, Yale University is today one of the world's preeminent centers for instruction, research, and public benefit. Over the years, its scholars have extended the pathways to knowledge. Yale is the guardian of the imagination that both defines and asserts our humanity. The Yale Campaign has few precedents. To succeed, however, Yale must have an unprecedented commitment from those who can best appreciate the

University's agenda . . . . Members of the Yale family have always been the trustees of this great treasure.

Yale University
New Haven, Connecticut

Closing Paragraph

Today this trusteeship falls to a new generation. All who know and love Yale will be called upon to participate with generous enthusiasm in the $1.5 billion program for The Yale Campaign.

Yale University
New Haven, Connecticut

The Fail-Proof Checklist

Here are questions to ask, examine, and review before starting your writing. Use it as a guide to complement what I've discussed in this book.

✔	**How Is the Institution Positioned in the Community, and What Is Its Heritage?**
	When was the institution founded?
	What were the circumstances surrounding the beginnings?
	What geographical area does the institution serve?
	Natural resources in the area?
	Industrial and business concentration?
	What distinguishes the area from the rest of the country, state, or nation—a capital, a distribution center, a rural area?
	Describe the population of the service area.
	Population trends. Increasing or decreasing? Aging?
	Level of affluence and occupational types?
	Educational level and cultural types?
	Ethnic origins?

✔	**How Does the Institution Benefit the Community—How and Whom Does It Serve?**
	What are the services offered by the institution?
	How many people use these services? Have they been increased or decreased? Why?
	How much do each of these services cost? Are they furnished free or subsidized?

	What are the services offered by other organizations in the institution's service area?
	Is there any duplication of services, or is the organization's niche unique?
	Does the institution cooperate with other organizations in joining programs or use of facilities?
	In the community, is there a need for services not currently being met that the institution could fill if it had increased funds?
	How many potential new users of the institution could you expect to attract if its programs were increased?

✔	**Why Is a Fundraising Program Necessary?**
	Why does the institution need funds?
	Is the program for capital or endowment or both?
	Specific components of the campaign and project?
	How will the campaign improve the organization's ability to fulfill its mission?
	How much money does the institution need?
	How will the money be raised?
	Have alternative sources of funding been investigated (government grants, bonds, etc.)?

✔	**Is the Institution Fiscally Sound?**
	What is the current operating budget?
	Is the institution operating in the black?
	Who makes the major contribution to the present operating budget?

	Does the institution have a membership drive, annual support campaign, admission fee, or subscriptions?
	Does it have an endowment?
	What are the financial assets and liabilities of the institution?
	Are the fees charged (if any) competitive?
	Does the institution have a planned giving program?

✔	**Does the Institution Have Strong Leadership?**
	What is the composition of the board of directors (or trustees)?
	How many are on the board?
	Are different ages and both sexes represented?
	Major business and commercial interests?
	Community minorities or institution's constituency?
	Is the staff well qualified?
	How many persons are on the staff?
	What are the major strengths and accomplishments of the executive director and other key staff?
	Does the institution use volunteers, and are they effective?
	Do the administrative facilities meet the requirements of the staff and volunteers?

The *CasE*valuator

There are many elements that must be included in a case statement. That's the mechanical and technical side of developing the material. But nothing takes the place of good writing. That's the creative side. You must prepare copy that sizzles—and states clearly and dramatically the need and urgency. Even a project that is unquestionably valid requires writing that has genius, magic, and power.

If the reader doesn't share your vision and isn't propelled to become a partner in your great cause—no matter how pressing the need, you haven't made the case. Period!

Don't be unduly concerned about the order. There are times that it's much more compelling to start with the vision.

And sometimes, historical facts and details about current services can be handled best as exhibits in an appendix.

What counts is that you don't leave anything unanswered or open to challenge. And yes, one thing more—that you end up with a case statement that represents the institution with style, grace, and integrity.

Use this ***CasE*valuator** to rate the twelve essential factors that determine the effectiveness of a successful case statement. Indicate the points for each item in the right-hand column. Total the points to score your case statement. Note that the rating of *Poor* is scored as *minus two* (–2).

The *CasE*valuator

1. Mission Is Stated or Interpreted for Easy Understanding
2. Brief History Explanation of why institution was founded and societal environment that existed at the time that impelled its creation
3. How Institution Provides Its Services Indication of constituencies served and statistics, explanation of activities, programs, and leadership
4. Institution's Vision for the Future Clearly and dramatically stated
5. Explanation of the Proposed Project Description and rationale of the items to be covered in the program . . . and the cost
6. Institution's Singular Role in Meeting the Need Indication of how institution is uniquely positioned to meet the need through the proposed project
7. Readability of the Copy
Exciting, memorable title
Compelling section headings
Theme (title) is woven through material
Reads easily
Brief, declarative sentences—mostly present and future tense
Short paragraphs
Strong, inviting opening statement
Powerful close, a call for action, theme restated
Emotional and dramatic copy

	Poor	Fair	Good	Very Good	Excellent	Points
	–2	4	6	8	10	

The *CasE*valuator *(continued)*

8. A Clear Sense of Urgency The project must move forward—it is one minute 'til midnight, and time will not wait	
9. Anecdotal Material Numbers and statistics have a place . . . but dramatic stories provide sizzle and make copy come alive	
10. Emphasis on Those Who Receive Service Focus is on the need and those served . . . not on the institution	
11. Focus on Reader Copy is reader-oriented . . . how the reader has a stake in the issue . . . and can help solve the problem	
12. Reader Is Asked to Share in the Vision Invitation is extended to become a partner in the program	

Scoring for the *CasE*valuator

165–200	You have an excellent case statement . . . compelling and urgent . . . clearly defined. You've made your case! Some fine-tuning will make it perfect.
140–164	You're well on your way. There is still some work required to make it precisely the case you need . . . but you don't have much more yet to do.
120–139	It's good—but not good enough. You'll need to review all of the items where you scored poorly . . . and make necessary additions and revisions.

	Poor	Fair	Good	Very Good	Excellent	Points
	–2	4	6	8	10	
				Total (This Page)		
				Total (Page 1)		
				TOTAL POINTS		

90–119 A *fair* case statement won't make the sale . . . you have major work to do to bring this up to high standards.

89 & Below Unacceptable . . . at times, it's easier to start over than to attempt a major overhaul. Don't be discouraged . . . but your draft can't be used in its present form . . . you have work to do.

About the Author

A fundraiser for more than four decades, Jerold Panas is the executive director of Jerold Panas, Linzy & Partners, which has more than 60 staff and has served over 3,500 organizations since its founding in 1968. During his career, he personally has helped raise an estimated $11 billion for a wide variety of charitable organizations, including many organizations around the world.

Panas is widely regarded as the foremost author on fundraising, having written or co-written 18 books on the subject, as well as countless articles for magazines, newsletters and newspapers around the world. One of his books, *Asking*, is the bestselling book in the history of fundraising, while others—including *Mega Gifts* and *The Fundraising Habits of Supremely Successful Boards*—are classics and standards for the profession.

Recently Panas was the recipient of the prestigious Chair's Award for Outstanding Service presented by the Association of Fundraising Professionals (AFP).

15 Brook Street – Medfield, MA 02052
Tel. 508-359-0019 – Fax 508-359-2703
www.emersonandchurch.com